Tears Of Mercy

By Crystal L Woods

Table of Contents

Mindful Meandering.......1

Powerful Presence.........23

The Salvage Yard..........29

Three Wishes...............37

A Warm Day in March...43

A knock at the Door......49

Prayer of Many............55

The Dream..................67

The Washroom............73

Confronting the Demons..81

Spiritual Gifts...............90

Timely Blessings...........101

The Test.....................106

Dark Days...................111

Relentless Rushes..........115

The Calling..................120

Power of forgiveness……126

Reflections………………130

Tears of Mercy (Poem)…132

Authors page……………..134

Psalm 51:17

The sacrifices of God are a broken spirit: a broken and a contrite heart, O God, thou will not despise.

Thoughts

Too often times, we as Christians get through the dark, un-favoring perils of our lives, make it through to bright sunny days and stop…we've forgotten about God.

We don't want others to know who we used to be, only what we've become…we've become shameful.

We get what we need to succeed, turn our noses to those who are trying to climb out of the mess they've found themselves in…we've become prideful.

We don't offer help, examples, "What we used to be", and "How with the grace of God I made it through." We've become selfish hoarders.

But, you have a voice. You have a testimony. Because you've overcome, your trial isn't yours anymore. Share it. Release it to give hope to the hopeless.

Dedication

I dedicate this book to my daughter and son. Always know that through the toughest of life's journey, a bit of faith will carry you for miles upon miles, a long way and the things that deem impossible to man are nothing that our, all too powerful, God can't handle. He has promised a way of escape and He alone can and will deliver you.

Acknowledgement

A special thank you to

Dr. Rose Marcia Metts, proofreader

To My Mom

She knew she could not even began to take on the daunting task of raising three daughters and a son without the guidance of her faith, church, friends and family.

Thank you for seeing to it that we always attended church and were involved in its functions. You laid our foundation and gave us something that no one could ever take away, your warm forgiving heart and the true gospel of our Lord and Savior Jesus Christ.

Tears of Mercy book and Tears of mercy (poem)

Library of Congress TXu 2-002-415

ISBN/ 978-0-692-80567-1 /USA/ All Scripture Quotations are taken from the Holy Bible: King James Version and are not owned by the author

Printed in the USA

The contents of this book are based on true events. Characters names are fiction.

Mindful Meandering

Cara lays under her Down comforter in the early morning hours, mildly searching her past but very present thoughts. No hurt or embarrassment this time, only thoughts fill the calm air. Starring straight-faced, underneath the bright glimmer of light that raced through the faux wood blinds of the bedroom window. A peaceful moment in solitude, she remembers past life experiences that had abruptly interrupted her world and left stripes of pain in her memory. She had survived somehow, some way with God's help. All the hurt and anguish was gone. No feelings of despair, just thoughts. No regrets of any kind, but very much grateful for having come through and making it this far. A calm disposition, instead of past uncontrollable anxiousness. Only peace and pondering of events that would mold and shape the woman she would become this day. A woman of character. A strong woman of Christ.

All those times before, Pastor Luca had mentioned spiritual growth and how to obtain, which didn't mean much at the time, she being in her early twenties. After all, she was married to her high school sweet heart John, good to family and friends and that had to carry some weight with God or so she thought.

It was a holiday, Presidents Day to be exact. Lying there all cuddled up alone, too cold to get out of bed, she begins to fade out of sorts and nod back off to rest some more. While the neighborhood lay quiet and still, she drifts back off into times past, remembering when…

Eight years into the marriage. It was year 2000 on a warm Sunday afternoon. My daughter Rhiannon, baby Will and I had just come home from attending church services with a co-worker who had first invited us as my last my last trimester of pregnancy approached. Just upon entering our small townhouse, the phone rang. It was John. He said he really needed to talk to me in person. It was important. I couldn't believe I answered, for I was able to ignore his calls for about a month now. I didn't want to be bothered before. I had a new baby boy to tend to and a seven-year-old daughter who was experiencing enough drama between her dad and me that she was misbehaving in school. I can still see her big brown eyes fill with tears as John and I would argue. It was all such a huge injustice to her innocence.

I agreed to see him. I didn't know why; it just felt okay to talk and listen to what he had to say. It was time for me to break my silence as well. The distance between us was good and allowed my mind to feel rested. I had no idea why he wanted to see me or what he would say. After all he had what he wanted and there was nothing I could do about that. The doorbell rang. I answered and there stood a tall, dark, handsome man who seemed lost, empty, like a gambler who had played his last loot after feeling so certain the hand he dealt would yield the greater gain.

Lots of things had entered my mind in the months prior. I was emotionally shaken to my very bones and felt like I was losing control. I often pondered thoughts of renting a small moving truck and leaving under the cover of night with the kids. I could have moved back to my hometown or to another state and started all over again. I was overwhelmed with hurt and fear. I even talked to my daughter's principal to find out how to transfer her. I was unstable in my thought process. I could have run as far away as possible, but I didn't. The words of my late father-in-law kept playing over and over in my head as he spoke to the many he had mentored. "You can't run from your troubles; they will find you wherever you go until you work through them." So with that, I chose to stay and deal with the mere ugliness of my situation and I mean it was ugly.

Satan continued to attack me at every angle because I was weak and he knew it. Many times during my pregnancy, John would come by the office where I worked and say the most hurtful, uncalled for things. I felt alone. The joy of my unborn child stretching, squirming and growing inside of me gave promise to new life and carried me through. Nothing else made sense. It was the same thing time and time again. John would stand back and stare at me after he accomplished getting me upset while customers waited in line for assistance. I always asked him to leave and let me work, but he seemed to get joy out of seeing me cry. The kind hearted man I once knew, who had once protected and cared for me, had turned into a monster, un-recognizable.

I lived in a town where I had no kin folk to lean on, but lots of associates from work who cared. They had become my family. Some had even gone through the very horrible things I was facing and assured me I wasn't alone.

Once a co-worker asked me was I "getting any" in front of the crew. I laughed out loud, but really wanted to burst into tears. She sensed my inner pain as I watched the look of, "(I just stuck my foot in my mouth)," written all over her face. But I wasn't mad. Things weren't going well at all. I just didn't realize how complicated things were at first or how difficult they would get. I was blinded and dumfounded to learn that my husband, the man I had trusted, was having an affair. These things happened to other people, or at least I thought.

Believe it or not, it came in a dream. I literally awoke early one morning crying, sweating and trying to fight my way back into full consciousness as I wrestled back and forth in bed. In my dream, I was standing face to face with a girl I had never seen before. She stared back at me with a mellow calmness, as if to say, "Don't you know?" She had long blonde hair and piercing blue eyes of confidence. When I awoke, I knew without a shadow of doubt, in my heart what my spirit was relaying to me. I would learn several days later, this girl who was a figment in the night, was in fact the other woman. No, I didn't eat a strange food or watch a disturbing movie that night; this was real. I called my mom and began to tell her of the revelation I'd had. Her exact words made me tremble inside. Gasping for air as she spoke, she said, "Cara, do you know what just happened? You had a premonition. God showed you this! Her reaction chilled me to the bone on top of the whirlwind of emotions I was already feeling. And with that, the mystery was solved.

My mind started to spin in reverse of events that had happened prior to the dream. Like the friend that John had pick up Rhiannon from after school care on his Friday to get her so that I wouldn't have to leave work early. I asked Rhiannon to describe the girl to me that came to get her. Her words haunted me and sent my heart pounding when she said, "Who, Christina?" She knew her and described her just as I had dreamed. I was even more taken.

The unordinary character John started displaying towards our moving into a more suitable place for the baby to be raised. I couldn't understand why he didn't move with us. We were a family. Now it all made reasonable sense. I had assumed he didn't move with us right away because he was mad that I had taken the "man role" and apartment shopped myself instead of making it a couple affair, but I couldn't have been more wrong.

And now he wanted to talk…

We went upstairs for privacy, out of the ear of our seven-year- old daughter. “Thanks for letting me come over,” he said. I walked over and sat on the foot of the bed where the mattress curves around. John began to kneel on the carpet a couple feet in front of me. His face had a bewildering shame all over it as I watched his eyes wonder and search for the right words to say. I had never known him to look this way before and still I had no clue as to what he would say next. “I’m sorry for everything I’ve put you through. You must hate me. If you do, I don’t blame you.”

“I don’t hate you,” I said.

“I hope you can find it in your heart to forgive me. Will you have me back?”

“Yes,” I said.

And just like that, my family was under one roof again. John and I started the process of trying to mend a torn relationship.

God had answered my prayer along with the group of girlfriends that joined my efforts in spirit nightly at 7pm. They were my prayer warriors.

Later that evening…

A guy called wanting to speak to John, but somehow I knew it was a cover for Christina. John looked at me for approval and I nodded knowing I could hear everything in our scarcely furnished, quiet little place.

"You broke my heart in a million pieces, how could you do this to me?"

All John could say was, "I'm sorry Christina, it's all my fault."

All the crying I heard her doing, over the phone, made me feel sorry for her. Sure she was wrong for knowingly getting involved with a married man, but somehow we had both fallen victim to John's games. She was hurting badly. On this day that John had asked me to take him back, he had moved out of her apartment and into mine while she worked to my unknowing.

As time passed, raising our daughter and son became priority. Things were slowly shaping up, but variant. John wasn't quite the same man I had married. He was different. The affair was still in his heart. He tried to hide it carrying about in normal everyday activity, but I could see the struggle in his eyes.

I remembered a friend once told me, "He's already been out there and got a taste; now it's going to be easy for him to get out there again."

I took what she spoke as truth because I knew of her adulteress pass life, as much as much as she confided to me, but I was still concentrated on doing my part to make my marriage work.

The upcoming year would prove hard. I suffered many unfair things. Strange comments and suggestions would lead me to believe he was comparing me to her. Once he ridiculed me for recording entries in my check book with black ink.

"Why can't you be different?" he said. Some people use an array of colors to represent different things."

I felt a little sick inside, but continued with my method. Not really sure if he was aware of how he made me feel. I was determined to just be me and no one else. I learned that emotional affairs just don't end at the drop of a hat. There's a process of healing that has to take root and because I chose to work things out with John, I would unknowingly become a part of the process. With the complication of it all, the girl in which John had been involved with moved four townhouses down from us with her new boyfriend. Talking about too close for comfort and one too many awkward run ins. I was a heart attack waiting to happen.

Then I began to ask God, "Why do I have to endure all these things I'm facing? What have I done to deserve this? Why does confusion seem to follow me everywhere I go?"

Like the time Christina and her boyfriend parked right beside me at the big box store and practically trotted up behind me so that they walk almost in "running into distance" only to slow up so I would have the lead again; as they both laughed. The hair stood up on the back of my neck, but I spoke not a word and kept being the bigger person. I often asked God for protection and then sometimes I just wanted to disappear. I wanted this whole ordeal to just go away. I even asked God to miraculously fix this trial and maybe give me a different one, but this cup wasn't passing. I had to go through all of it, whatever that would mean. In time, I learned that God is no respecter of persons and my attitude gradually changed to, "Why not me?" As mysteriously as the girl appeared in my dream, and a few run ins to boot, she would vanish the same way. Never to be seen again.

I desired to be a strong woman of faith and soon accepted that the harsh things I endured was part of the path laid to get me where I needed to be in Christ. Satan was a spectator in the marathon of life that I raced and believe me, he showed up at every mile only to taunt me. He said things like, "You loser, why don't you just quit. You're not going to win. Why don't you just give up and go home?" I had to continue to speak out loud and shake him loose. "GET BEHIND ME AND LEAVE ME ALONE. YOU HAVE NO PLACE HERE. IN THE NAME OF JESUS." I became bolder and more courageous to fight the labels and thoughts of destruction. Eventually time would heal. My husband also became the man I once knew again. Our love would prove to be stronger than it had ever been. It all came with a price. A nice hefty sum. A breaking down of self-wills and the picking up of one's cross.

Three years passed. We purchased a house and moved two towns south of where we were living. Things were continually falling into place. I myself learned to trust a little, relax and love deeper, but to never put John above my Savior. I told God to never send me a trial such as the one I had faced.

"Give me something else to prove long-suffering and loyalty towards you."

Who was I to tell Him what to do and communicating to Him in this way? But I did as I pleaded with Him how I didn't want to feel the again pain that adultery causes.

For the most part, I was grateful. We had been given a second chance. Some of the reasons for my sufferings from my husband's indiscretions were soon realized. Somewhere in the beginning of our marriage, I had placed my utmost trust in John and forgot that only God and He alone should hold that type of rank. John was a natural man, whom I loved without question, but God was perfect in every way and could never fail me. I had placed Him on the back burner and had forgotten about Him.

Then He lead us to the first couple we would witness to about His plan for forgiveness and reconciliation. The amazing thing was, these were people who knew nothing of our past and somehow thought we were the perfect couple, had it all together until we shared otherwise. We were being used for a much greater purpose than ourselves. God was being glorified through these works and that was the bottom line. God had my undivided attention and I made a promise to never leave Him again no matter what test would come my way.

In 2005 John and I were invited by a neighbor and his wife to be a part of a series of classes they were hosting at a local church along with other couples. The class was on, "How To Affair Proof Your Marriage." We joined the Wednesday night classes with much humility. While no one shared recovering from an affair, John's past sin remained a secret in the back of my mind. I managed to keep it all tucked away safely. John and I agreed to keep moving forward. In that same year, we all met at a local coffee shop and renewed our vowels in the presence of a minister. God was working and mending my heart, but Satan never gave up on his goal to quietly slip back in and destroy our family.

- 1 Peter 5:5 Likewise, ye younger, submit yourselves unto the elder. Yea, all of you be subject one to another, and be clothed with humility: For God resisted the proud, and giveth grace to the humble.
- James 1:2-4 My brethren, count it all joy when you fall into divers temptations; knowing this, that the trying of your faith worketh patience. But let patience have her perfect work, that ye may be perfect and entire, wanting nothing.
- 1 Peter 5:8 Be sobor, be vigilant, because your adversary the devil, as a roaring lion, walketh about, seeking whom he may devour:

Thought… Saints remember while we are in our affliction, He is afflicted. He will never leave you alone.

Powerful Presence

Seven years later, a cool day in December, end of another year. Bright transparent rays streaming through the side glass entry way of the house. Yellow and purple violas align the pots by the front porch. Will watching cartoons on the computer. Giggling sounds fill the living area. It's Saturday, wash day, the one chore I don't mind doing. In fact I really get a lot of satisfaction in cleaning things up and putting them away, make me feel complete in a way.

A co-worker once said to me, "Yes, I was like you when I first started. I thought I was going to clean the world of defaced and raggedy money, by daily muting, but you'll get tired soon and you'll start circulating some of that money right back out."

In making my way room by room, I hear Rhiannon's voice, from her open bedroom window, in the back yard talking to the dog as if he was a real person. So funny, she loves that dog. One basket at a time, I take the dirty clothes down to the washer and back for another. John leaves for the hardware store. "Cara, I'll be back", he yells while pulling the front door behind him. Carrying about in a content way, I continue on with my chores as an inspirational song fills my head and drowns my cares away. When all of a sudden, out of nowhere. I heard a voice say, "Don't leave" as I walk without a care, past the refrigerator, to the wash room with the last basket of dirty laundry in tow. My hairs immediately stand up on the back of my neck as soldiers reporting for duty. It stopped me dead in my tracks because no one else was there. Just me. Suddenly I felt surrounded by a presence. A safe place. I cautiously turned and looked to my right because that was the direction in which the voice came from. Nothing but some appliances staring back at me. It caught me off guard, as if it lay in wait for me to pass by that very moment. "I know that's you Lord. Whatever it is, I won't go," I mumbled under my breath, having no idea what was transpiring as I smile a cheapish grin in between somewhat startled and assurance. Soon a calmness rested over my entire body and I wasn't afraid. It was like everything around me had frozen still for just a moment. Like, I had entered a tranquil aura of sorts. I cautiously made my way down the brick steps to the washroom and rested the basket against the dryer and thought, "Lord, what just happened and what does it mean? I know you'll reveal it to me."

I hear the truck pull up outside and I meet John at the front door to tell him what just happened.

"Wow, what do you think it could mean?"

"I don't know", I say as he walks right past me with little concern.

During the next few weeks, my lightened steps were as if I was walking on air, but normalcy of life would weigh me back down and I would leave the encounter I had a distant memory.

- Samuel 3:4b That the Lord called Samuel: and he answered, Here am I.
- Ephesians 5:19 Speaking to yourselves in psalms and hymns and spiritual songs, singing and making melody in your heart to the Lord;
- Isaiah 26:3 Thou wilt keep him in perfect peace, whose mind is stayed on thee: because he trusted in thee. Psalm 46:10 Be still, and know that I am God: I will be exalted among the heathen, I will be exalted in the earth.

Thought… Always reverence God, acknowledging His authority every time you come to Him, no matter the cause.

The Salvage Yard

Two months later, Tuesday evening. John comes to my job.

"Cara, I met these two guys in the corporate meeting today. They're from Columbia. We started talking about old cars and they're into the same stuff I'm into. I pulled out my pictures of the kit car and we got to talking. They told me they know where an old junk yard is close by their houses and we plan on getting together Saturday morning if that's okay with you."

"Who are they?" I ask.

"Mike and Roger, I showed them pictures of my old kit car and they're sure I'll be able to find parts for it in this huge salvage yard."

I looked at John strangely because I felt something was up. “We’re doing well, aren’t we?” he said.

“We’ve been doing well for years now. You don’t have anything to worry about.” John sounded good, but something didn’t add up. I felt suspicious about the trip, like he was hiding something, but I went along with it anyway.

“You trust me right?” he asked as he kissed me.

“Okay, what are the names of the guys again?”

“Mike and Roger, Mike said I could stay with him and you can call me if you need to. Only thing is, I would like to leave on Friday night, make the two hour trip as soon as I get off work, stay over Mike’s house and since the yard opens up at 10:00am we can go on over and have the early part of the day looking around and I could plan on heading back home Saturday evening and be home before dark. Well, let me get back to work and we can talk some more tonight.”

Thursday night, I was in the bedroom getting ready for bed when John came home from work.

“You still feel okay about me leaving on Friday?”

“Yeah”, I said.

“This might be the place where I finally find some pieces I’ve been looking for.”

Friday, just before closing time at work. John picks Rhiannon and Will up from afterschool care and dropped them off at my job. He was all packed up and ready to get on the road. I’ll call you when I get to Mike’s house, okay?”

“Okay.”

The kids and I pulled out of the parking lot and follow in behind him up the road a piece.

My cell phone rang. It was John. “Where y’all headed?”

“We’re going to get some dinner,” I replied.

“Oh, just don’t have the kids out too late, okay?”

“I won’t”

Friday around 11:00pm, I called John to see if he had made it okay.

“I’m here, just a little tired.”

“Okay, I love you.”

“Me too”, John said.

I felt a little unsettled, but prayed as usual and fell off to sleep.

Sunday came and John wasn’t home. He said he was too tired to drive back Saturday evening. Will went to a college basketball game / birthday party with his best friend and some of the other kids from the neighborhood. Rhiannon and I made it a girl’s day and went out shopping and had lunch. John called and said his trip was unsuccessful and that he would be back in town in about thirty minutes. Several unanswered calls to his cell, the hours passed into the night. I got the kids ready for bed because it was late and they had school the next day. A car pulled in the driveway. It was John.

"Sorry, I stopped to get gas and ran into some guys close by the house and got carried away talking."

He reeked of cigarette smoke.

"Your hair smells like cigarettes and it's really bad."

"Is it that bad?"

"It's unbearable."

"Yeah the guys I was talking to were smoking." He got out of bed and washed his hair. John's life was on a runaway train, but I just didn't know it at the time. I didn't want to believe it, but some of the signs were there.

- 2 Thessalonians 2:3 Let no man deceive you by any means: for that day shall not come, except there come a falling away first, and that man of sin be revealed, the son of perdition.
- Romans 2:16 In the day when God shall judge the secrets of man by Jesus Christ according to my gospel.
- Hebrews 4:13 Neither is there any creature that is not manifest in his sight: but all things are naked and opened unto the eyes of him with whom we have to do.
- Psalm 40:4 Blessed is that man that maketh the lord his trust, and respected not the proud, nor such as turn aside to lies.

Thought… Through every trial, praise Him from beginning to end.

Three Wishes

March 2007, Friday evening, 6 o'clock couldn't come soon enough. Interesting e-mail hits our inboxes at work. Make three wishes. Think of something you want to happen today, tomorrow and the day after it read. Before we left the building we started naming different things and having fun with it. As for me, well everyone knew I wanted to be a stay-home-mom someday and had been praying and seeking God on the matter for some time. There were wishes of money, vacations and silly things that we all laughed about. I had been praying and trusting God for three years straight, without wavering, "Lord I don't know when it's going to happen or how, but I'm trusting it will because I know you can do anything."

When Rhiannon and Will were babies, I needed to work outside the home to keep my sanity and balance, but things were different. They were growing up so fast and I started feeling like I was missing out on being there and sharing in all their new ventures in school. Working a 9 to 5 had gotten old. It left me tired and exhausted most of the time, and there was not much more of me left during the week after the work day ended. I was tired of the game, the game of wake up, get myself ready, then get the kids ready for school, work all day, pick up the kids, come home to cook, get baths and on to the same old thing again while trying to juggle wife to John. Turning wife and mother on and off was a daunting challenge at times. Never much time for me and every time we would leave on a Friday to go on an out-of-town trip, my anxiety level would rise to near panic: watching the clock to ensure we got back on the road at a decent time, to make it back home at a good hour, so that we all got enough rest in for the school day and work day ahead. I was "job scared"

I was giving all my energy to work and my family got very little of me. Something had to give. It was time. I was ready for the Lord to rescue me somehow. I was at a stale place where I longed for new things in my life as well as for my family. I was burnt and felt John didn't appreciate me and all I did.

I remembered a conversation that a girlfriend and I had while taking a break at work. We shared with one another on how our spouses took us for granted. Would they even care if they came home and found that we had packed up all our belongings and left? I fantasized about climbing the tallest tree and capturing John's initial reaction at finding me disappeared.

- Proverbs 3:3 Let not mercy and truth forsake thee: bind them about thy neck; write them upon the table of thine heart:
- Hebrews 12:28 Wherefore we receiving a kingdom which cannot be moved, let us have grace, whereby we may serve God acceptably with reverence and godly fear:
- 1 Thessalonians 5:17 Pray without ceasing.
- Philippians 4:6 Be careful for nothing; but in everything by prayer and supplication with thanksgiving let your request be made known unto God.

Thought… Know that God is perfectly capable of rendering your every need.

A Warm Day in March

A nice warm day in March lures some of the families on our street out to enjoy and share in the summer-like weather. The smell of freshly cut grass intertwines with the sounds of children playing. Sheila and Trent take what would be their last stroll up and down the road before the birth of their twins would come. Nothing like a gorgeous day to bring an easy smile to everyone I encounter. I wave as they walk by in a slow pace. "I'm sure glad my baby days are over", I think as she slowly but surely make it back down to her home.

"They wanted babies and now they're having babies" I mumble under my breath. "Good people, those two."

I erect a homemade table on the front lawn by setting up two sawhorses and placing a large sturdy piece of plywood on top. Time to stain some of the new floor molding I've been putting off for a while. Piece by piece, I place the pre-cut, numbered pieces on the table and began staining in coats. John pulls in on his motorcycle, hops off and runs inside to drop off something and pick up pamphlets for and upcoming event to take to some of his customers who will be attending. I get on his cycle and pretend I'm riding as he walks back out of the house.

"Get off", he says with no wager whatsoever and off he goes. Out of the corner of my eye, I see my neighbor pull in across the street in his truck. I finish staining the wood and put some things away before heading back inside. I leave my project still damp outside to soak up the last warm rays before the sun goes down.

I go to my bedroom and gaze upon the new mattresses we had purchased and delivered this morning. In looking all around and thinking on my day, I am reminded of how blessed I am. I can hardly wait to sleep on the new mattresses. My day has pretty much ended with the thoughts it couldn't have been much better, with the exception of a neighbor frustrated with Will and another boy losing a part to his son's shooting toy in their backyard. With Will upset and my not knowing the best way to deal with the situation, I call John for advice, and he heads back home at my request.

- Psalm 9:1 I will praise thee, O Lord, with my whole heart, I will show forth all thy marvelous works.
- Matthew 5:16 Let your light shine before men, that they may see your good works, and glorify your father which is in heaven.
- Romans 14:22 Hast thou faith? Have it to thyself before God. Happy is he that condemneth not himself in that thing which he alloweth.
- Psalm 113:3 From the rising of the sun unto the going down of the same the Lord's name is to be praised.

Thought…Store up the beauty of God for the days of sorrow.

A Knock at the Door

I hear a gentle tapping at the door. It's probably one of Will's friends, I thought. No, that's someone else.

"Is your mom here?"

"Mom, someone needs to see you", Will said.

I go to the door and find one of my neighbors standing there. It was Tess and she had a worried look of strange reluctance on her face. Her hair was wet and she looked as if she'd come straight over from getting out of the shower. "Cara", she said, whispering every word carefully, "Jake just came home from the mall and said there's been a bad wreck up the road. He got out of his truck, and walked over to the scene because he thought it looked like John's motorcycle. His suspicions were confirmed when he saw it was John. He told me to come straight over and tell you. "It's really bad and they've taken him to the hospital. What are you going to do?"

I asked if she knew which hospital. Good thing Jake had asked an emergency worker where they were taking him.

"Send your kids over to my house and you go check on your husband."

The tears immediately came rushing down my face as she embraced me. At that moment I had become the recipient of bad news and uncertainty, but somehow I was able to quickly dry my eyes, take a deep breath and pull myself together before going back inside. I couldn't get the kids upset. I couldn't let them see me crying. I had to be strong.

"Rhiannon, Will, I need both of you to go to Mrs. Tess's house for a while. I need to go help your dad with something, Okay?"

They both knew something wasn’t right, but without a question, they went.

- Proverbs 27:10b For better is a neighbor that is near than a brother far off.
- Esther 4:3 And in every province, whithersoever the kings commandment and his decree came, there was great mourning among the Jews, and fasting, and weeping, and wailing, and many lay in sackcloth and ashes.
- Ephesians 6:1-2 Children, Obey your parents in the Lord: for this is right, Honor thy father and mother, which is the first commandment with promise;
- Leviticus 19:18 Thou shalt not avenge, nor bear any grudge against the children of thy people, but thou shalt love thy neighbor as thyself: I am the Lord.

Thought…be an empathetic Christian, always praying for others.

Prayer of Many

On the way to the hospital, I knew I needed to get my family praying with me. I was in a place where I'd never been before. Running off of pure adrenaline, I started calling everyone I could think of. I basically, one by one, told them all the same thing.

"John was involved in a bad motorcycle wreck. I'm on my way to the hospital now. I don't have any details yet, but I'm just calling because I need for you to start praying, now!" Everyone was so supportive.

The hardest call to make was to John's mom, Ruth, my mother-in-law. She lived alone in another state and had already suffered the loss of a husband and two daughters. John and his older brother were the last remaining siblings, and she often expressed her concerns about John owning another motorcycle with two young children to rear.

It was a long drive, on a Saturday evening, in a tourist driven area in spring. Finally I pull up to the hospital and play musical cars before I find a place to park. Briskly walking through the automatic doors, my eyes make contact with the attendant. She stood up as soon as I came in. Almost as though she was expecting me and knew I was the family member to the injured motorcycle victim. Before I could finish my sentence, "This way", she says directing me to his room. My view was tunneled as if she and I were the only people present. My mind scrambled back and forth to, what if he's gone? No he's fine, but what if?, what would I say or do?

My heart rate started to rise so much that I could feel it beating in my ears. I began to walk pass the open and closed curtains in the ER rooms of patients waiting to be seen for various reasons. All I wanted to do was get to him, but I was in a fog and everything around me seemed to be moving in slow motion including me. I finally get to his bedside, and there he lay. He was very much alive. I immediately lock my hands in his.

Looking over to me, squinting in pain to open his eyes, he said, “You’re here, I can’t believe you’re here.”

“Why wouldn’t I be here? I’m your wife,” I thought.

His statement made no sense at all. Why wouldn’t I be here? Quickly dismissing it, my entire body shrugged a huge sigh of relief. Thank God, he’s alive. Obviously in agonizing pain from all the moaning and groaning sounds coming out of his mouth from a deep unknown source inside of him. I watched one side of his chest rise well above that of the other in a matter of moments. Something was bad wrong. I’d never witnessed anything like this before. The doctor asked me to stay in the room while he and the nurse whisked John off for x-rays to the second floor.

A police officer was there waiting to speak to me. I could feel his eyes pressing against me and was aware he had been standing by the entire time. He cautiously came in the room with me.

“How are you doing ma’am?”

“Oh, just trying to hang in there.”

“Are you the wife?”

“I am.”

“I’m sorry for all you’re dealing with right now, are they saying he’s going to be alright?”

“Yeah, the doctor said he believes he’s fixable.”

The officer nods his head and says, “I’m glad to hear that.”

“I hate to trouble you with this now, but I just need to ask you a few questions, if it’s alright?”

"Oh, sure."

"Were you at the accident?"

"No, a neighbor of mine saw the scene of the accident and had his wife come to the house and tell me."

"Okay. Is the bike insured?"

"Yes, but I can't think of the name right now. I can see if I have something in my truck outside."

"Oh no, that's fine. Has he been drinking tonight?"

"No, he doesn't drink alcohol."

"Okay, well thank you ma'am and I hope everything works out for you."

"Thank you."

When the officer left, my mind began to scramble again. I was afraid they might not bring him back to the room. "What if he dies? Then what will I do?" I was visibly shaking. While my emotions try to get the best of me, they wheeled him back in the room where I waited. The x-rays revealed a broken rib cage and a collapsed lung. The doctor assured me that John was going to be fine. I needed to hear that. I was relieved. The nurse on duty gave me a plastic bag to put his belongings in while we waited for his pain medicine to kick in and an available ICU room.

Kneeling down, I started with his bloody jeans and leather jacket that were cut off of him at the scene of the wreck. Memories started flooding my mind. I bought the leather jacket seventeen years ago, when we dated, as a birthday gift. Now it was all cut up, but it was only material and I was just glad to have him alive. When I squatted down to retrieve his wallet and cell phone, he asked for his phone.

"You don't need your phone", I told him.

He said, "I need to check it."

“No, you won’t be making any phone calls for a while.” I placed it in the bag along with the other items. He told me he loved me and the kids. I told him everything was going to be alright, just try to rest. He worried that I would leave him at the hospital alone.

“Please stay”, he said.

“I’m not going anywhere, I wouldn’t leave you”, I told him.

The medication had showed its position when, out of nowhere he started talking to one of his friends, I mean a friend that wasn’t there. I asked him did he really see this person.

“He’s right over there. Don’t you see him?” he said.

I started to laugh. Laughing felt good. John was hallucinating. Seconds later, he dozed off to sleep and started snoring only to wake up every few minutes and ask some of the weirdest questions. Like,

“Abraham Lincoln’s the president, right? And my brother is 80 years old?”, when he was really forty-four. Then off he went to snore some more.

John always made me laugh when we first met in high school. He was a regular funny guy. It was the second thing that attracted me to him besides his good looks.

- Proverbs 3:5 Trust in the Lord with all thine heart;and lean not unto thine own understanding.
- Revelations 8:4 And the smoke of the incense, which came with the prayers of the saints, ascended up before God out of the angel's hand.
- Psalm 9:11 Sing praises to the Lord, which dwelleth in Zion: declare among the people his doings.
- Ephesians 6:18 Praying always with all prayer and supplication in the Spirit and watching thereunto with all perserverance and supplication for all saints.

Thought… Never suffer alone. Coming together as one to the almighty serves as strength.

The Dream

Three days after the wreck I awoke crying in a cold sweat. Another nightmare that felt so real. My heart was pounding and fear surrounding me like a tight glove. Evil was present. "Go get his cell phone." It was strongly on my mind as if I was craving a particular food and had to have it for satisfaction. I got out of bed and slowly walked through the living room to John's desk. There lay his phone. My hands were shaking like two leaves on a windy day. My heart felt like it was going to jump out of my chest. I picked it up. It was locked. Okay, I thought. What could the password be? Then I remembered a combination of numbers he had used on other things in the past. I put them in and much to my surprise, they worked. I couldn't believe how easy it was. And there it was in plain view, right in front of my eyes. The evidence of a double life. It was happening all over again, another affair.

The last text he sent out was only minutes prior to the wreck to her, the nameless person on the other end of the chat. I grabbed a chunk of my arm and squeezed tightly. I wanted to believe I was dreaming and all this was wrong, but I was wide awake. The cold tile against my bare feet assured me and chills echoed from my sweat drenched chest. I needed to breathe, but struggled greatly to do so. Tears refused to come, only a dry ache. My chest, legs and arms began to hurt simultaneously. I thought I was dying. Staggering down to the wash room, with my arms pressed against my guts, I quietly close the door behind me so not to awaken the kids. I wasn't quite sure what to do with myself or what lead my feet to this room. A strange unfamiliar place it seemed as I look wide eyed from the washer to the door in a blank stare. Crouched over and confused as to whether I should stand or sit. I needed relief, but it was nowhere near. Sitting down on the vinyl topped concrete floor, I embraced my arms with my right hand squeezing the left and the left squeezing the right. I started to rock back and forth with my legs criss-cross, like an orphan child neglected in search of comfort in the midst of abandonment. My right fingers easily make their way parting through my stroked hair. I stood up for relief for my body knew not what to do with itself. Turning to the wall, I softly pound my closed fist against it. Turning back around, I rest my back against the wall and slid down to the floor. I got on my knees and lay in a fetal position. I pound both fist against the floor when a sound came out of me like the start of a release of pressure and soon after another disturbing embellish until I could no longer contain the hurt locked inside. I lay in deep despair and wept a hopeless puddle of immense misery.

- Daniel 4:5 I saw a dream which made me afraid, and the thoughts upon my bed and the visions of my head troubled me.
- Psalm 55:4 My heart is sore pained within me: and the terrors of death are fallen upon me.
- Psalm 62:8 Trust in Him at all times; ye people, pour out your heart before him: God is a refuge for us. Selah.
- Acts 2:17 And it shall come to pass in the last days, saith God, I will pour out of my spirit upon all flesh: and your sons and your daughters shall prophesy, and your young men shall see visions, and your old men shall dream dreams:

Thought… Talk to a Christian adult who can offer advice and personal experience.

The Washroom

"God please help me. I'm hurting so bad. It's happened again. I don't know what to do. What do I do? Help me! Please Lord! I need you now."

3:00 a.m., I call Pastor Luca. All he could hear at first was sobbing. I made several attempts to identify myself, but he couldn't understand me.

"Calm down", he said in a mellotone voice.

I was able to for short periods of time, enough that he finally recognized who I was. I told him of the findings on John's phone. "Help me please!" I was desperate. "Tell me what to do."

"Oh Lord, not again sister", he said. "This is bad!. This is real bad!"

The advice he gave me was anything less than conventional. "I need for you to listen to me", he explained. "You have two major things going on in your life right now, and they need to be address one at a time. I know you're hurting, but you need to somehow put this on the back burner for now and work on what's at hand. Satan wants you to lose your mind at this point, but you have to hold yourself together. You can't back down. Go to the hospital like you have been normally. Ask your husband, 'Is there anything I can do for you?' Comb his hair, brush his teeth, feed and bathe him. These things are important because he is helpless in his body. Show him kindness. Wait until the end of the week when he is better, and only then do you address the affair."

“How in the world am I going to do this?” I asked. I thought my pastor was crazy. “How in the world could I stay quiet about something so detrimental?”

“You can do this. I know you’re going to get through this”, he said.

I couldn’t think straight, but he had to know what he was talking about. After all he was my pastor for fifteen years and surely he had heard it all over his many years in the ministry and had been a sinner himself before coming into the safety of Christ. The one man I needed to trust.

“God please help me to be a good servant during this very difficult time. I don’t know how to do this, but give me the strength I need for today, In Jesus name I pray, amen.”

The next couple of hours passed so quickly and just as usual in my distress, I somehow pulled myself together in time to get Rhiannon and Will up and ready for school. Having no sleep at all, I had no choice, but to keep going. I put the kids on the bus and drive to the corner convenience store for a soda and newspaper. The clerk at the store offers her concerns for John and says that everyone is thinking of him.

“We didn’t know until Sunday about the wreck”, she explained. “How is he doing?”

“In bad shape”, I tell her.

“Let him know that we are thinking about him”, she says.

“And you are Michelle?”, I say while my eyes focus in on the small typed font of her nametag. “Okay, I’ll tell him you asked about him.”

She walks out of the store behind me, rest her back and foot against the brick wall on the front of the store and lights a cigarette and off I go on my daily commute to the hospital to check on John.

I make my way to him and sit on the chair at his bedside. A preacher that had fallen from grace was the headlines on the local news with confessions of doing drugs and prostituting while in the ministry. I looked over to John from the wall mounted television in front of us. Maybe he'll confess to me of his own misconducts, but I got nothing, not even a twitch of the eye. I wanted to know what he was thinking, but I couldn't tell. I wasn't God. John was very social and well liked in our community and it showed. The next few days would yield many visitors to his bedside, whether they be young, old, male or female, they came and through it all he gave no clue to his inner demons. God saw me through several days without revealing to him what I knew. He allowed my heavy heart to be put to the side and take care of his broken body.

- Psalm 9:13 Have mercy upon me, O Lord; consider my trouble which I suffer of them that hate me, thou that liftest me up from the gates of death.
- Romans 10:13 For whosoever shall call upon the name of the Lord shall be saved.
- Psalm 119:71 It is good for me that I have been afflicted; that I might learn thy statutes.
- Psalm 120:1 In my distress I cried unto the Lord, and he heard me.

Thought… Find a quiet place in your home where you can get into the presence of God without distractions.

Confronting the Demons

It's been almost a week now. The doctor has moved John from intensive care to a regular room. After many conversations with my pastor, I feel confident that I can handle what's about to transpire. Today is the day. Anticipation is growing. It's time to confront the demons. It's time to tell John that I know what he's been up to. I start to feel sick to my stomach. I tell him,

"You've got something going on in your life that you need to get right with God."

He looks at me very hatefully and says in a mean tone, "You don't know what's going on with me. You don't know anything about me."

I was thrown for a loop. I couldn't believe he had the audacity to get so defensive with me when he was the one clearly at fault. I came undone at the sharpness of his words. I was disappointed in myself because I was able to hold it together for almost 7 days and now it all unravel too quickly. I had left my body armor, sword and shield at home. Evil showed up in him like a bat out of hell and I was caught completely off guard. I wasn't prepared for the conversation to go the way it was headed. I began to lose control.

"I won't be here to take you home when you're released in the morning. Let her come," I said. Now he knew that I knew. "I'm not doing this again with you. I can't do this. If I hadn't found out you were cheating, this could have gone on for years."

"You're probably right", he said with sarcastic confidence.

I felt even lower, humiliated. Then he suddenly seemed remorseful. Only because he was caught and had nowhere to run to, I suppose. It was him talking out of his pain. Then he started to cry so I made a demand.

“If you want your family, call her right now, in front of me and tell her it’s over.”

“I can’t remember her number”, he said.

But I had memorized it the instant I saw it on his phone. Those numbers were photographed in my brain. I handed him my cell and ratted off the numbers and he dialed just as sure as I was standing there.

“She knows”, he said, “She’s right here. Listen, It’s my fault. I take all the blame.”

But, I wasn’t satisfied, so I stepped outside the heavy, private hospital room door, paced up and down the hall while I got her on the phone and demanded to know her name. John wouldn’t tell me. She wouldn’t budge either. I could tell by the cautious way of her words and tone that she was nervous and someone was near that she didn't want her conversation heard.

"I wash my hands clean", I said. "If you want him so badly, come and get him. He's being released in the morning."

"That wouldn't be a good idea", she said.

I was so frustrated, I terminated the call. My phone rang back, but I didn't answer. Later, I listened to the voice mail. It was her. She yelled, "That b---- didn't answer her phone" as if someone was with her that she needed to sound big to. I told John about the obscene message she left.

He said, " No, she wouldn't say anything like that."

That confirmed to me that he was really messed up, in this thing really deep. He was taking up for her. I felt so disgusted. I literally wanted to throw up, for I had heard these similar words before. Seven years ago to be exact. At that point, I felt it was a lost cause. It was a bad night with no resolution. The accomplishment was anger. I get back on the road for the lonely drive back home and cried myself to sleep.

- Ephesians 6:11 Put on the whole armor of God, that ye may be able to stand against the wiles of the devil.
- 1 Corinthians 15:58 Therefore, my brethren, be ye steadfast, unmovable, always abounding in the works of the Lord, forasmuch as ye know that your labour is not in vain in the Lord.
- Ephesians 6:12 For we wrestle not against flesh and blood, but against principalities, against powers, against the rulers of the darkness of this world, against spiritual wickedness in high places.
- Psalm 6:2 Have mercy upon me, O Lord; I am weak: O Lord, heal me; for my bones are vexed.

Thought… We're all given a moment, a small window of time, to respond rationally in a difficult situation. Use that moment and choose to react in a wise way, otherwise you are acting in self and self never gets you far, just in trouble.

Spiritual Gifts

After facing the initial trauma of learning that I was indeed not the only woman in John's life once again, I would go through the agony of my mind racing during sleepless nights. If I didn't put my utmost hope in the God I was serving, this ordeal would consume me. I was better and stronger than that. I cared about myself and what would become of me. I kept telling myself, "Relax, you've survived this before and whether you stay with him or leave the marriage, you can make it through once again." It wouldn't be easy. Satan was fully aware of my relationship with his rival and he knew what could hurt me more than anything. He attacked at every angle possible of what seemed like every waking day. When no one was home or when I'd be in my car alone, I would cry out loud to God. "I NEED YOU LORD! HELP ME TO MAKE IT THROUGH TODAY. GIVE ME A WORD OR SEND SOMEONE TO WITNESS TO ME." I would then start to thank Him with the mention of whatever came to mind. I was adamant that Satan wouldn't destroy my will to continue to serve my God. It was so important to bless God with my mouth. By this, many wonderful things would enter me and I would often cry tears of joy. In return, God was showering down "TEARS OF MERCY." I realized no matter what had transpired in my life, God was showing me mercy and I needed to count my blessings. If I hadn't experienced these trials and tribulations and allowed God to bring me through to the other side, I would have never known this amazing feeling of His rescue, His comfort and His joy. Praising Him became a daily event as I hurt. I was indeed growing more and more in God's grace. There were many challenging days were I struggled to speak audibly to God, but instead would praise Him in tears with my face to the floor and magnify His name.

On outings strangers would appear and say the most intriguing things. I knew it had to be words orchestrated only from God himself. Close friends and family often spoke of, "What a strong woman I was for God and my family." At those times I realized He was carrying me.

One day, while feeling a little speechless and tired, I mustered up enough strength to go grocery shopping. I parked my car in the store's parking lot and sat there for a while listening to some uplifting music. A moment later, this lady comes up to car with a huge loving smile. I crack my window and she slips a small pamphlet to me that read, "GOD'S PLAN FOR MARRIAGE."

Another incident would come on a day of fasting. I went down to the local DMV to renew my tag and the lady behind the counter says to me, "You're a Christian, aren't you?" My weak eyes lit up as I confirmed with a nod. She then said, with a peculiar tone, “You’re fasting and whatever you’re going through, don’t give up, you’re going to make it.”

If that wasn’t powerful, I don’t know what was. Strength from out of nowhere leaped into my physically drained body and perked me upward with confirming confidence. I was amazed that she would converse with me in this way. She was not only taking a chance of getting reprimanded by her employer if heard, but most importantly taking a stand for the Creator.

Time and time again I would come to know that God was always close because I continued to draw near to Him. Even when I didn’t know how or what I was doing, amazing things continued to happen.

At some point I knew I needed to try a different tactic to falling asleep at night. The powers of darkness would try and steal me, especially at night when my body and mind slowed to rest and time was idle. I read scripture after scripture on subjects pertaining to my need. Nonetheless, didn’t seem to aid me in resting. I began to think about an elder at church, when I was younger say, "If you keep your mind on Him, you will be in perfect peace." This became my motto verse for life and even in my thoughts, I found myself reciting it all the time. I thought, "If I keep my mind on Him, there was no room for the ever evil that tried to break me down."

A television evangelist often told his congregation, "You have to replace those bad thoughts with good ones."

One night I went to bed, got in a comfortable position, closed my eyes and continually spoke the words, "Thank you Lord" in my mind. I was in a zone where nothing else mattered. When all of a sudden, My hands raised up, my body felt as though I had been lifted from the bed and the deepest part of my belly belted out of my mouth a tongue. On both sides of me where all these voices and tongues that began to speak at the same time I spoke. It was truly amazing. I couldn't see the other people, but knew they were present because I could clearly hear them. I was drawn in so quickly and so strongly that it went on and on for what seemed a long period of time. God stood directly in front of us. Although I couldn't clearly see Him, His presence was so powerful. He spoke not a word. He only stood calmly to receive our praises. Then the spirit started falling off of me like an echo and as it left; I was slowly lowered back down to my bed. My heart started to pound as I came back into the natural realm. I opened my eyes and quickly sat up in bed looking all around the room. I had come back from a spiritual high. A new place, a place of Utopia where God dwelled. My heart was pounding as I breathed heavily.

John awoke and asked, "Who were you talking to? I couldn't make out what you were saying."

"I was speaking in tongues, talking to the Lord."

"Oh that's good", he said and dozed back off to sleep.

I lie back down and reflect on the event. God had filled me with His Holy Spirit, His supernatural power. What could this mean exactly? Whatever it meant, I knew I wanted this every day.

As soon as the morning light shown through, I could hardly contain myself anymore, so, I called many to tell of my experience. One person was skeptical and asked was I sure it was God, but everyone else was astonished and basically said the same thing, "Gods preparing your mind and body, making you stronger to fight the enemy."

The best place in my life I had ever visited would be this day and so it would be that I took a leap and crossed over to much more that God had for my life for Him. My strength would be renewed supernaturally, praying to God in the spirit. Now I understood fully why some of the saints in the church sought after God in this way, as much as He would give.

- Mark 16:17 And these signs shall follow them that believe: In my name shall they cast out devils; they shall speak with new tongues.
- Psalm 150:1 Praise ye the Lord. Praise God in His sanctuary: Praise Him in the firmament of His power.
- 1 Corinthians 14:2 For he that speaketh in an unknown tongue speaketh not unto men, but unto God: for no man understand him. Howbeit in the spirit he speaketh mysteries.
- Isaiah 40:31 but they that wait upon the Lord shall renew their strength; they shall mount up with wings as eagles; they shall run, and not be weary; and they shall walk, and not faint.

Thought…The Lord wants to take you to new heights and depts In Him.

Timely Blessings

Having John home from the hospital was a daunting challenge. I felt that it was too soon for him to be released, but the doctor saw otherwise. Rhiannon and Will were both very happy to have their dad home. I myself was relieved that his life was spared. I had no idea what I was getting into when it came to caring for him. I was exhausted. The week behind me and all its displeasures had left me twenty pounds lighter and with very little energy. Friends and neighbors were unbelievably generous. Family after family came day after day with prepared meals so that cooking would be the least of my worries. The next few weeks we received so many blessings, things that hadn't crossed my mind before. At one point while Will was vigorously sorting through a truck load of groceries a neighbor had brought by, he asked, “Why is everybody bringing us all this food?” It was the perfect opportunity for me as his mother to teach him that people have lots of good things in their hearts and when someone they know is hurt, they reach in their heart and take out those good things to show others how much they care by giving. I was amazed at the outpouring of love that was continuously being shown to our family. Cards, gift cards, flowers and quality time spent with our family, kept me upbeat and my mind off of the affair. Through it all, God was showing us His mercy. We continued to be blessed.

When the company died down, I began to think of John’s deceased father and how I wished I could talk to him one more time. He was the only man who could turn John on a dime with his wisdom. He was a true man of God. Oh, how I missed our conversations. John longed for him as well. During a conversation John and I had with a couple we had befriended, we were led to a revelation that our blessings were coming from not things we had done, but from generational seeds John's father had sown for his off springs. It all made good sense. God never stopped amazing me. Through my obedience to do the will of God, it was like He was saying, "Well done, my good and faithful servant, I'll never leave you. I'll see to it that you have what you need. I will take care of you."

- 2 Corinthians 12:9 And he said unto me, my grace is sufficient for thee: for my strength is made perfect in weakness. Most gladly therefore will I rather glory in my infirmities, that the power of Christ may rest upon me.
- Psalm 126:5 They that sow in tears shall reap in joy.
- Romans 12:12 Rejoicing in hope; patient in tribulation; continuing instant in prayer.
- Psalm 46:10 Be still, and know that I am God: I will be exalted among the heathen, I will be exalted in the earth.

Thought… Be able to receive blessings from others just as well as you are able to be a blessing.

The Test

At some point in my marriage when John and I were a young couple, I asked God to give me a warning, a sign or something to alert me of trouble that was approaching and He always did just as I had asked. At times when I was closest to God I could hear and discern quickly and clearly. At other times of my walk, I'd become a little too relaxed and things seemed to fly over my head, though He always revealed things I needed to know, whether I was paying attention or not.

When things got quiet at our house and returned back to somewhat normal, is when Satan lurked to see which angle he would be more affective with me. During these times, I also learned that the store clerk, who had offered her concerns for John while he lay in the hospital, was the other woman and she too would move into close proximity to our new home with her boyfriend, soon to be husband. Months passed by and John health improved. I strategically planned my next move. I decided I would leave. End the marriage. The affairs had taken a toll on my health and I could never trust John again. He started to cry and plead with me for this not to happen. "You'll see, he said. "I'm going to make it up to you."

With much praying and talking things through, we decided that I could resign from my job and become a stay-home-mom. It was all surreal! At that moment, everything God was preparing me for began to flash across my mind so vividly: It all began to unfold. The day I heard the words "Don't leave", while making my way past the kitchen to the wash room. The revealing nightmare I had when John was in the hospital, and the ceaseless praying I'd done asking God to be a stay-home-mom. It had become as clear as crystal, my breakthrough had finally arrived, right there in front of me, but it didn't come nicely wrapped like I imagined it would. All I had to do was grab it. I was so close to blowing it, ruining something I put a lot of time and effort into. Now God was saying, “Here you are Cara, the desires of your heart.” This horrific ordeal, I’d experienced would unbeknownst at the time be my test.

- Titus 3:3 For we ourselves also were sometimes foolish, disobedient, deceived, serving divers lust and pleasures, living in malice and envy, hateful, and hating one another.
- Matthew 9:28 And when he was come into the house, the blind men came to him: and Jesus saith unto them, Believe ye that I am able to do this? They said unto Him, Yea, Lord.
- Isaiah 61:3 To appoint unto them that mourn in Zion, to give unto them beauty for ashes, the oil of joy for mourning, the garment of praise for the spirit of heaviness; that they might be called trees of righteousness, the planting of the Lord, that he might be glorified.
- Luke 1:37 For with God nothing shall be impossible.

Thought… Ask yourself, where will my test lead me in Christ?

Dark Days

I faced some ridicule from family and friends. “Divorce him”, was the more common approach I received, but I had certain soundness with myself in knowing I had kept my vows and stayed faithful. I truly loved this man and although he had broken our circle, to me this was the “For Worse” I’d taken with the promise I’d given unto death parted us.

I received my breakthrough, but the devil still wanted me to break down and crumble. Things didn’t change overnight in my fight against the power of darkness. I faced many a dark day. I wanted to know for sure if John was capable of cheating again somewhere down this thorny road of happiness, and the answer was inevitably “Yes.” The sure thing was, I now wanted to stay in my marriage, therefore I had to abate the idea of fully trusting John and put my total utmost trust in God. All of my young life in the church, I would hear, "Don't let the devil steal your joy." I was too determined not to let that happen. To allow that would be doom. Thirteen years ago, I'd asked God to give me "quick recovery." This would become a crucial role in my getting through dark days. My logic was: I have to live here on Earth for a time and during my stay I'll experience unbelievable distressing situations. The key was to not allow my sorrow to wear out its welcome, then Satan would be more than happy to oblige. Satan wanted me at my weakest state of mind.

- Hebrews 13:3 Remember them that are in bonds as bound with them; and them which suffer adversity, as being yourselves also in the body.
- Romans 5:3 And not only so, but we glory in tribulations also: Knowing that tribulation worketh patience;
- Job 13:15 Though he slay me, yet will I trust in Him: but I will maintain mine own ways before Him.
- Romans 12:19 Dearly beloved, avenge not yourselves, but rather give place unto wrath: for it is written, vengeance is mine; I will repay, saith the Lord.

Thought… Don’t ever stop communicating with God; especially while in your suffering. Crying your way through prayer will only allow the trueness of your heart to overflow in his ears. He wants to meet you right where you are.

Relentless Rushes

I became a detective when John returned back to work. I needed to take control or so I thought. I found myself reaching for receipts and small pieces of paper out of the trash to investigate their manner of business. Many times I would question John on things I'd come across. Everything had to have a legitimate explanation. The overwhelming feelings of anxious searching left me desperate and unsatisfied. I realized I had to stop. This wasn't a part of God's character. John's adultery had affected me in the worst self-conscious way possible. I was a cool, calm person before any of this and I wanted to know that person again. My actions to hold him accountable in every small way had brought me to near ruin with the strong hold it had upon me. The thirsty need to snoop had reshaped my innocent ability to benefit any ones doubt.

The only way to escape this drug-like behavior was to pray, fast and ask God to take the desire to do so far away from me, and He did, but it wasn't instantly. I had come to the understanding that I had no control over John's life; only he did and whatever he did wrongly out of my sight, well God knew about it. The fact of the matter was, I wasn't trusting God, but rather telling Him He wasn't capable of handling my situation. If things were to work out in my favor and for the good of me, I would have to take care of me and trust God. I would have to place my unbarring troubles at his feet and leave them there.

The constant arguing over the years left me exhausted and burned out. I had wasted entirely too much time fighting a fight that wasn't mine. It belonged to God. Through it all I continued to seek God and my purpose for this life. Some that knew me and my story saw a drab unfixable situation, but year after year I became a soldier for the Master, picking up pieces of armor for readiness and meditating on the lesson plans I needed for graduation. I was being groomed for stewardship, something much larger than I could imagine.

- James 1:12 Blessed is the man that endureth temptation: for when he is tried, he shall receive the crown of life, which the Lord hath promised to them that love him.
- James 4:4 Ye adulterers and adulteresses, know ye not that the friendship of the world is enmity with God.
- Galations 5:16-17 This I say then, walk in the spirit, and ye shall not fulfill the lust of the flesh. For the flesh lusteth against the spirit, and the spirit against the flesh; and these are contrary the one to the other; so that ye cannot do the things that ye would.
- Galations 6:9 And let us not be weary in well doing: for in due season we shall reap, if we faint not.

Thought… In all that you do, stop and ask, "Is this the will of God?"

The Calling

During the course of my life with John would present a series of dreams. I recall the first one occurring our first year of marriage. While sitting at the breakfast table with his mom and dad, he began to tell of a dream he had.

A voice said to him, "Let me show you the way." He and an unknown person walked for what seemed like days through tough terrain up and down hills. They could see a small light flickering in the distant, but could never seem to come within reach of it. As they got to the end of the path they were traveling on and to the top of the hill, the light shone so brightly that you could barely look at it. The traveler said to him, "This is it." He turned to the traveler, but he had vanished, and all around him was empty pews.

I began to giggle by how John was telling this dream to us, but his dad (a true man of God) was startled by the account and said to him, "Sounds like you need to get some things right with God."

Eighteen years later and shortly before John accepted His calling, he would have another strange occurrence that awoke him from sleep. One morning he was very shaken and asked me if I saw the figure last night standing at our bedroom door. I never saw anything, but John described it as a large, dark figure holding what appeared to be a reaper in his hand. I knew at this point, time was running out for him.

I remember John and I casually talking to couple from out of town, at a local mall, while we stood in line waiting to be checked out. The gentleman paid for his purchases ahead of us and in turning to leave, calmly turned back and shook John's hand as he addressed him as "preacher" while nodding. We turned to look at each other in question as he and his wife walked away. It was truly another confirming moment because John was dressed in regular clothing and never mentioned God's name in conversation with the couple. There was no doubt in both our hearts that John was called to do a mighty work for God. It was all too clear, do or die, and finally he did. That would be the last thing revealed to him before he told our church bishop and began working alongside him studying God's word. John's acceptance into the ministry would be the best thing that had ever happened to my marriage. I began to look at him in a different light. John was not for me to worry over anymore; now he belonged to God.

- Romans 10:14-15 How then shall they call on him in whom they have not believed? And how shall they believe? And how shall they believe in him of whom they have not heard? And how shall they hear without a preacher? And how shall they preach, except they be sent? As it is written, how beautiful are the feet of them that preach the gospel of peace, and bring glad tidings of good things!
- Hebrews 11:6 But without faith it is impossible to please him: for he that cometh to God must believe that he is, and that he is a rewarder of them that diligently seek him.
- Psalm 51:17 The sacrifices of God are a broken spirit: a broken and a contrite heart, O God, thou wilt not despise.

- Jonah 1:1-2 Now the word of the Lord, came unto Jonah the son of Amittai, saying, Arise, go to Nineveh, that great city, and cry against it; for their wickedness is come up before me.

Thought…Listen, God is speaking through others to confirm what He has already told you.

Power of Forgiveness

Forgiveness wasn't something I'd experienced completeness with, with the women and all the disruption to my life over the years. There was no way I could obtain this on my own, but through He who is perfect; God the Father. My life had been an emotional roller coaster. Because I was a fleshly, living, breathing, human being, I could feel the sting of pain. The years of wearing my heart on my sleeve lead to hurt, rejection and betrayal. At times I would retreat, hide, close up and use the knock downs to control how much I was willing to love or not love John. Every time I used these measures, a small voice would nag at me and say, "What are you doing? Jesus never launces out how much he is willing to love you, He just does."

Also knowing how disobedient I'd been in the past to Him and how much He has forgiven me. He loves in spite of and if I didn't forgive, the unsettled inhabitations would attach to my insides and harbor there. I needed to release the garbage. The trash was at the point of build -up and making me sick. It was time to empty the recycle bin and choose to live free. I asked God to forgive me and help me forgive. I fell on my knees and confessed to The Lord. I was ready to lay all the past and present pain at His feet and how I needed Him every second of the day to maintain just what I had asked Him until I could see past me.

- Hebrews 10:23 Let us hold fast the profession of our faith without wavering; (for he is faithful;)
- Acts 26:18 To open their eyes and turn them from darkness to light, and from the power of Satan unto God, that they may receive forgiveness of sins, and inheritance among them which are sanctified by faith that is in me.
- Colossians 1:14 In whom we have redemption through his blood, even the forgiveness of sins:
- Matthew 9:6 But that ye may know that the Son of man hath power on earth to forgive sins.

Thought…Understanding how and why God has forgiven you, helps you to forgive others.

Reflections

Well, they say three times is a charm. Mine would be in the strangest of ways, with the stripes of honor to prove it. One might say I'm crazy, another might say I'm a strong woman of God. Strong I am, courageous, firm and honorable, all these and more in my father's eyes.

The difficult displeasures that have tried to consume and overwhelm me, are more than I care to mention, have only pushed me closer and stronger right into the arms of Jesus.

I chose to forgive, forgive all who had betrayed me. I needed to be free and weightless from burdens that had held my heart captive for too long. I also chose to pray that salvation would find my enemies and free their heart as well. I am constantly reminded of Jesus's never ending love for me every single day I live.

Tears of Mercy (Poem)

All my days of dancing with the grieving clouds

circling in and out about the smoky illusions

wandering how I made it coming and going

my face appearing sometimes in full array

my limbs seen only with the light of day

shines a hue to uncover my whereabouts

you gave me tears of mercy

your warmth awakens the senses at heart

to mend the stiffness that plants itself to bones continually aging

when it seems I cannot do or go another step

you show me a different cause of why I'm here.

you gave me tears of mercy

when troubles all seem to come my way

and darkness wants to steal my day

you never left me in all of this

at times I want to turn and give up this battle

for it's your will, to do or don't

your words prepare and take me in

you gave me tears of mercy
your tears attach themselves one by one to form a covering
and softly whisper down and lay upon your child in need
safety and care covers the chill of nakedness
I can stand with boldness
You gave me tears of mercy

By Crystal L Woods

About the author

Crystal Dawn Little Woods was born in Lincolnton, NC to Viola L Metts and Buford R Little.

She now resides in Murrells Inlet SC with her husband Shawn, daughter Hannah and son Samuel. In her spare time, she enjoys spending quality time with her family, writing, knitting, singing, gardening, sketching and encouraging others to reach their greatness in Christ.